WORLD'S SCARIEST PREDATORS

PREDATORS OF
Asia and Australia

Amelia Madison

Cavendish
Square

New York

Published in 2015 by Cavendish Square Publishing, LLC
243 5th Avenue, Suite 136, New York, NY 10016

Library of Congress Cataloging-in-Publication Data

Madison, Amelia, author.
Predators of Asia and Australia / Amelia Madison.
pages cm. — (World's scariest predators)
Includes bibliographical references and index.
ISBN 978-1-50260-176-6 (hardcover) ISBN 978-1-50260-175-9 (paperback) ISBN 978-1-50260-174-2 (ebook)
1. Predatory animals—Asia—Juvenile literature. 2. Predatory animals—Australia—Juvenile literature. 3. Predation (Biology)—Juvenile literature. I. Title.

QL758.M34 2015
591.53—dc23

2014024982

Editor: Kristen Susienka
Senior Copy Editor: Wendy A. Reynolds
Art Director: Jeffrey Talbot
Designer: Douglas Brooks
Senior Production Manager: Jennifer Ryder-Talbot
Production Editor: David McNamara
Photo Researcher: J8 Media

These photos are used by permission and with the courtesy of:
Alamy: 16 (Amazon Images), Dreamstime: 8 (Lajos Endredi), 12 (Hotshotsworldwide), 12 (Crystal Taylor),
13 (Smellme), 20 (Hotshotsworldwide), 24 & 25 (Mathes), 28 (Bernhard Richter), FLPA: 16 (Gerard Lacz), 17 (Mitsuaki Iwago),
24 (Kevin Schafer), 28 & 29 (Michael & Patricia Fogden), Getty: 4 (Earth Imaging),
Photos.com: 8 & 9, Photoshot: 20 & 21 (NHPA/ANT).

Printed in the United States of America

Contents

Did You Know?

Asia is the largest, most diverse continent on Earth. Australia is the world's smallest continent, with unique wildlife.

Introduction

There are so many animals in the world, and each **species**, or kind, of animal has its own characteristics. Some animals have stripes, some are one color, and others use **camouflage** to protect themselves. Some animals are fearsome animals that we would not like to meet on a hike or in our backyards. Others are harmless and fun to observe up close.

Asia and Australia have some of the most interesting animals on the planet, including wild cats, **marsupials**, crocodiles, and snakes. Some of these animals have large claws to hunt with, while others wrap their bodies around animals they want to eat.

This book will reveal many incredible facts about some of Asia and Australia's scariest and most interesting animals. Remember that animals live nearby, no matter where you live. They are best observed from a distance.

Siberian Tiger

Scientific Name: *Panthera tigris altaica*

The Siberian tiger is the largest cat in the world, and can measure 11 feet (3.3 meters) long. Its huge head and powerful jaws are built for grabbing **prey**, snapping necks, and crunching bones. Although it may be large, the tiger is fast. It can run at speeds of up to 50 miles per hour (80 kilometers/hour) over short distances, but it prefers to hunt silently for its food. Creeping through the undergrowth, the tiger waits for prey to come close before pouncing on its victim. It will eat any available food, even bears! When young, tiger cubs live with their mothers. There are six cubs to a litter, but only a few make it to adulthood.

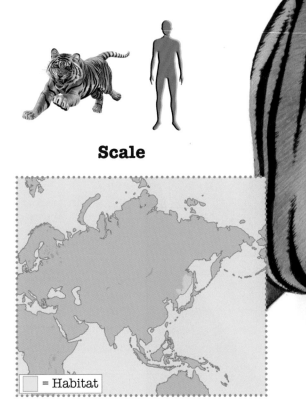

Scale

= Habitat

Where in the World?

Siberian tigers are found mainly in Siberia, Russia, around the Sikhote-Alin Mountain region and in the southwestern Primorye Province. Small populations also exist in China and North Korea. There are an estimated 400 to 500 living in the wild.

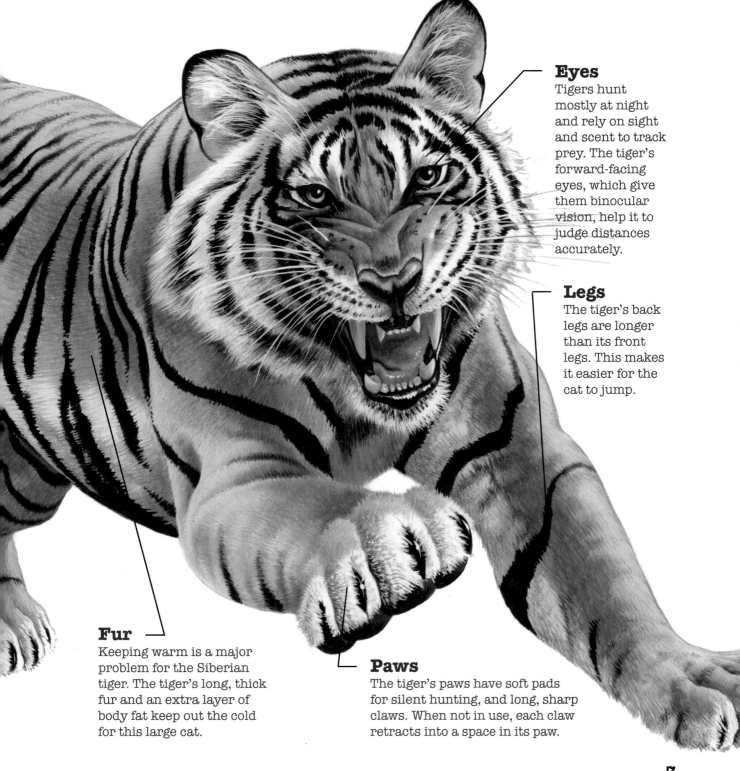

Eyes

Tigers hunt mostly at night and rely on sight and scent to track prey. The tiger's forward-facing eyes, which give them binocular vision, help it to judge distances accurately.

Legs

The tiger's back legs are longer than its front legs. This makes it easier for the cat to jump.

Fur

Keeping warm is a major problem for the Siberian tiger. The tiger's long, thick fur and an extra layer of body fat keep out the cold for this large cat.

Paws

The tiger's paws have soft pads for silent hunting, and long, sharp claws. When not in use, each claw retracts into a space in its paw.

Siberian tigers have
thick fur to combat
cold weather.

A tiger's canine, or front, teeth can grow between 2.5 and
3 inches (6.35 to 7.62 cm) long.

Ferocious Fact

Siberia covers around
77 percent of Russia, or
10 percent of the world's
landmass. Much of the
ground in this region stays
frozen for months. To keep
warm and give their bodies
energy, Siberian tigers need
to eat around 20 pounds
(9 kilograms) of meat a day.

When tiger cubs are born they have no teeth and depend on their mother for survival.

Siberian tigers have lost over 40 percent of their habitat in the past decade.

Tasmanian Devil

Scientific Name: *Sarcophilus harrisii*

Scale

Tasmanian devils are strong, stocky **scavengers** that hunt mostly at night or in early morning or evening. Although they mostly live alone, they prefer to eat together. Their shrill cries attract other devils to them. Early European settlers were so alarmed by the deep growls and fierce personality of this marsupial that they named it the Tasmanian "devil." It will eat almost anything, including road kill. However, the devil is also a ferocious **predator**. Its strong jaws give it one of the most powerful bites of any animal its size. Its long whiskers and excellent sense of smell allow it to track down prey in complete darkness.

= Habitat

Where in the World?

Once found throughout Australia, Tasmanian devils now live only on the island of Tasmania. Unlike most animals that live in very specific habitats, devils are found all over the island, although they prefer **scrublands** and forests.

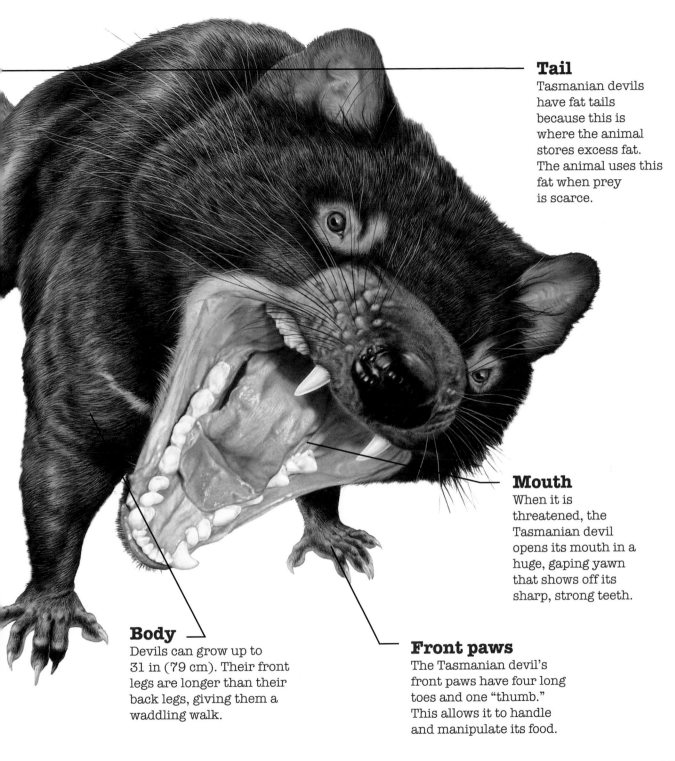

Tail
Tasmanian devils have fat tails because this is where the animal stores excess fat. The animal uses this fat when prey is scarce.

Mouth
When it is threatened, the Tasmanian devil opens its mouth in a huge, gaping yawn that shows off its sharp, strong teeth.

Body
Devils can grow up to 31 in (79 cm). Their front legs are longer than their back legs, giving them a waddling walk.

Front paws
The Tasmanian devil's front paws have four long toes and one "thumb." This allows it to handle and manipulate its food.

Tasmanian devils are carnivores that eat other animals for food.

Tasmanian devils have jaws that are stronger than a dog's four times their size.

Ferocious Fact

The Tasmanian devil's scientific name means "Harris's meat-eater." This greedy devil will eat any meat, including birds, snakes, and even human corpses, although its favorite food is wombat. It will store any excess calories as fat. One devil can eat up to 40 percent of its own body weight in meat in just half an hour!

Tasmanian devils often search for food killed by other animals.

Did You Know?

- The Tasmanian devil was the inspiration for a well-known Looney Tunes cartoon character called Taz.

- Tasmanian devils run at speeds up to 22 mph (35 kmh) for short periods, but they can keep up a pace of around 7 mph (11 kmh) up for several miles.

- Young Tasmanian devils are called pups, joeys, or imps.

- Tasmanian devils like to keep their dens very clean. They regularly change out wet or old leaves for new, fresh bedding.

Tasmanian devils are good at spotting moving objects but have more trouble when something is standing still.

Platypus

Scientific Name: *Ornithorhynchus anatinus*

With an otter's body, a beaver's tail, and a duck's bill, the platypus is one of the world's most unique animals. Although it lays eggs, it is considered a mammal, because it feeds milk to its young. It uses its entire body to power through the water, and its bill scoops up food on a river bottom. On land, a platypus moves awkwardly, but in the water, it is a dangerous predator. Its fur is thick and waterproof, allowing it to stay warm even in cold freshwater streams. It also has a stinger, or spur, on the ankle connected to a poison sac, making the platypus a venomous mammal. Its bill can detect changes in pressure and small electric fields given off by living bodies.

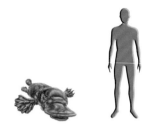

Scale

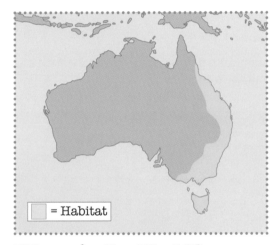

☐ = Habitat

Where in the World?

These strange animals are one of Australia's most famous inhabitants. They are found in eastern Australia and Tasmania, ranging from cold, mountainous regions to tropical rainforests. They dig homes called burrows in low-lying riverbanks, hidden by hanging vegetation.

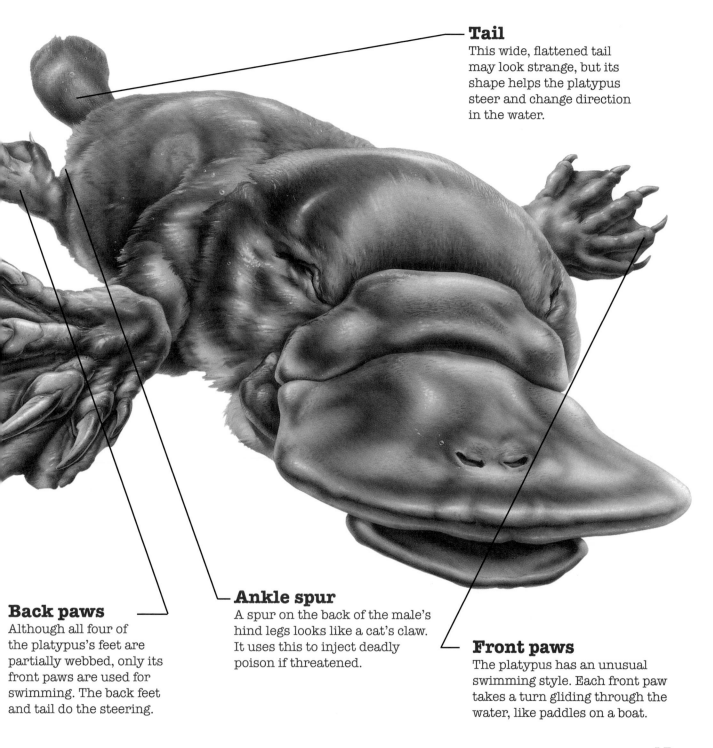

Tail
This wide, flattened tail may look strange, but its shape helps the platypus steer and change direction in the water.

Back paws
Although all four of the platypus's feet are partially webbed, only its front paws are used for swimming. The back feet and tail do the steering.

Ankle spur
A spur on the back of the male's hind legs looks like a cat's claw. It uses this to inject deadly poison if threatened.

Front paws
The platypus has an unusual swimming style. Each front paw takes a turn gliding through the water, like paddles on a boat.

A platypus looks like a mix between a duck, a beaver, and an otter.

Ferocious Fact

In 2013, a fossil of the largest known platypus ever to walk the Earth was discovered in Riversleigh, Australia. Based on the fossil, scientists estimate it was one meter (3 feet) long—twice the size of the platypus today. The existence of this fossil challenged the belief that there was only one species of platypus.

A platypus is a graceful swimmer.

Did You Know?

- The platypus is blind and deaf when hunting. It relies on its bill to detect worms, insects, and crustaceans to eat.

- Platypi do not have teeth. They scoop up gravel with their food and, at the surface, use the rocks to help them "chew."

- The first Europeans to see a platypus's skin believed it was a fake animal.

A platypus uses its bill to find prey.

While a male platypus might look cute, it is a poisonous creature.

Ghost Bat

Scientific Name: *Macroderma gigas*

The ghost bat is Australia's only meat-eating bat. It feeds on anything from other bats to small birds. A skilled flyer, it is easily able to catch prey in the air by using **echolocation**. However, it also attacks animals on the ground by dropping on its victim from above, wrapping them in its wings, and killing them with a bite to the head or neck. Once a kill has been made, nothing goes to waste. Ghost bats eat everything—bones, fur, feathers, and skin. Usually, these mammals live in communities called colonies, inside caves or dark areas. During the day, ghost bats rest, coming out at night to hunt.

Scale

= Habitat

Where in the World?

The ghost bat is found only in Australia. These large bats are found in northern Australia, western Australia, Queensland, and the Northern Territory, but they are becoming increasingly rare because of humans mining in their habitats.

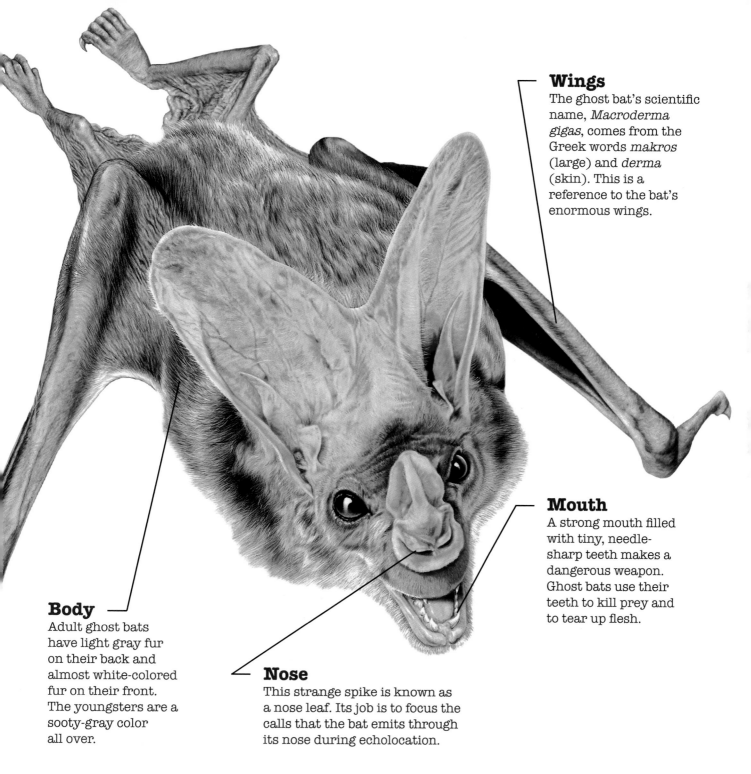

Wings

The ghost bat's scientific name, *Macroderma gigas*, comes from the Greek words *makros* (large) and *derma* (skin). This is a reference to the bat's enormous wings.

Mouth

A strong mouth filled with tiny, needle-sharp teeth makes a dangerous weapon. Ghost bats use their teeth to kill prey and to tear up flesh.

Body

Adult ghost bats have light gray fur on their back and almost white-colored fur on their front. The youngsters are a sooty-gray color all over.

Nose

This strange spike is known as a nose leaf. Its job is to focus the calls that the bat emits through its nose during echolocation.

Ghost bats are the only meat-eating bats in Australia.

Ferocious Fact

Ghost bats perch while hanging upside down. If a human did this, it would require a lot of energy and muscle power to get a good grip and hold on to a surface. Bats, however, have adapted to an upside-down existence that allows their muscles to relax rather than tense up while holding on to objects.

Ghost bats have thin skin on their wings and bodies that make them look see-through.

A ghost bat swoops down on its victim, a moth.

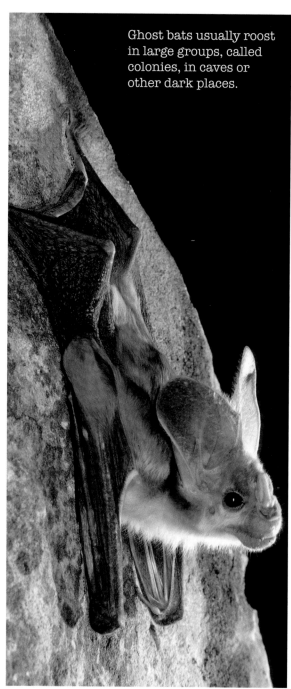

Ghost bats usually roost in large groups, called colonies, in caves or other dark places.

Did You Know?

- The ghost bat is also called the "false vampire bat" because it eats its prey like a vampire, and it was once thought to suck blood.

- Bats are the only mammals capable of flight.

- Female bats give birth to one pup each year.

- Young ghost bats begin flying when they are only seven weeks old. At three months old they are ready to start eating meat!

Mugger Crocodile

Scientific Name: *Crocodylus palustris*

The mugger crocodile is a patient predator. It spends most of its time in freshwater rivers and streams, waiting for food to draw close. Although it will happily hunt fish, the mugger is capable of grabbing an animal the size of a deer from the riverbank and dragging it into the water with its powerful jaws. Since crocodiles cannot chew, they drown large animals and store their bodies underwater until they begin to rot. This makes it easier to tear the carcass apart. This powerful reptile has fantastic eyesight, strong jaws, and can swim at almost 8 mph (13 kmh). It will even hunt on land, waiting near well-used forest trails for prey to pass by.

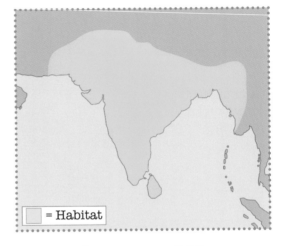

☐ = Habitat

Where in the World?

These fearsome crocodiles are found throughout the Indian subcontinent. They are a freshwater species and prefer slow-moving water. They can be found in man-made canals and reservoirs as well as rivers and marshy areas.

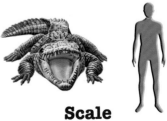

Scale

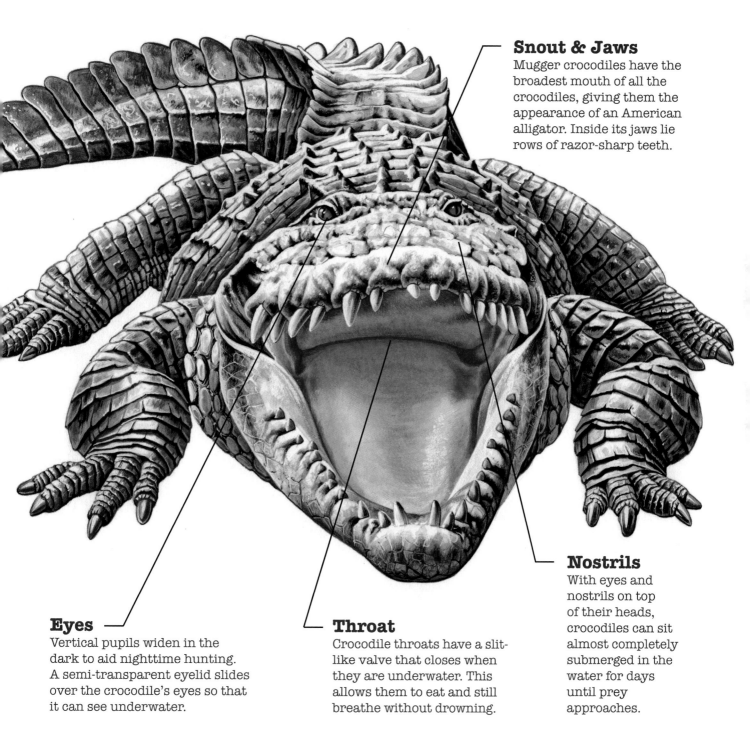

Snout & Jaws
Mugger crocodiles have the broadest mouth of all the crocodiles, giving them the appearance of an American alligator. Inside its jaws lie rows of razor-sharp teeth.

Nostrils
With eyes and nostrils on top of their heads, crocodiles can sit almost completely submerged in the water for days until prey approaches.

Eyes
Vertical pupils widen in the dark to aid nighttime hunting. A semi-transparent eyelid slides over the crocodile's eyes so that it can see underwater.

Throat
Crocodile throats have a slit-like valve that closes when they are underwater. This allows them to eat and still breathe without drowning.

Crocodiles cool themselves off by opening their mouths.

Ferocious Fact

Usually, it is easy to tell an alligator and a crocodile apart. Just look at their noses. Alligators have rounded, U-shaped snouts with broad jaws. Crocodiles have longer, more pointed, V-shaped snouts with weaker jaws. The mugger crocodile, however, has a broad, flat snout, making it look more like an alligator than a crocodile.

A crocodile has over sixty teeth in its powerful jaws.

A mugger crocodile is a massive predator that can harm any animal in its way.

A group of crocodiles is called a bask or a float.

Russell's Viper

Scientific Name: *Daboia russelii*

Russell's viper is one of the world's most **venomous** snakes. Identified by three rows of reddish-brown spots outlined in white along its back, its warning signs are a tightly coiled body resembling an S shape, the rearing of its head, and a hiss. In one bite it injects massive amounts of poison—up to 112 milligrams, which is more than enough to kill a human. Although they are **carnivores** and usually attack rodents and other small animals, if humans threaten it, Russell's viper will strike, and without help, its bite could be fatal. Like most snakes, this viper eats its prey whole. To do this, its jaws flip open on "elastic" **ligaments**, while muscle ripples force its victim's corpse down the viper's throat.

= Habitat

Where in the World?

These colorful vipers are widespread throughout most of the Indian subcontinent as well as China, Taiwan, and Indonesia. They generally avoid rainforests and marshy areas, but will occupy any other habitats where food is plentiful.

Scale

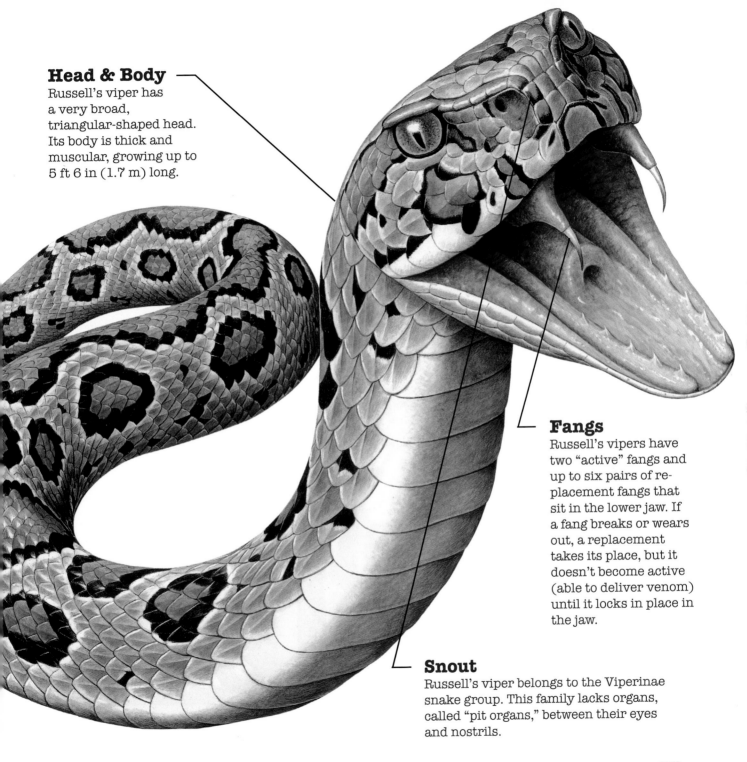

Head & Body
Russell's viper has
a very broad,
triangular-shaped head.
Its body is thick and
muscular, growing up to
5 ft 6 in (1.7 m) long.

Fangs
Russell's vipers have
two "active" fangs and
up to six pairs of re-
placement fangs that
sit in the lower jaw. If
a fang breaks or wears
out, a replacement
takes its place, but it
doesn't become active
(able to deliver venom)
until it locks in place in
the jaw.

Snout
Russell's viper belongs to the Viperinae
snake group. This family lacks organs,
called "pit organs," between their eyes
and nostrils.

Ferocious Fact

Russell's vipers can camouflage their bodies to blend in with their surroundings. Because they live in dry, grassy areas, the viper appears almost invisible. This is a type of camouflage called crypsis. Other animals in the world use mimesis, where they mimic other animals. With crypsis, Russell's vipers can remain hidden to its prey.

A Russell's viper's venom is so strong it can clot human blood in seconds.

The Russell's viper has unique colors that help it hide from predators.

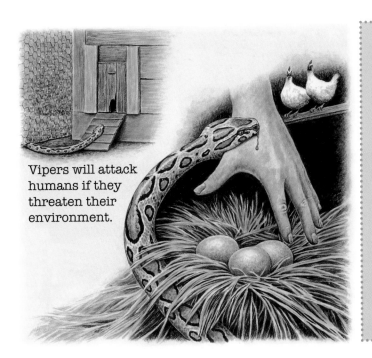
Vipers will attack humans if they threaten their environment.

Did You Know?

- Russell's viper is named after the Scottish naturalist Patrick Russell (1726–1805), who did much of his work in India.

- Russell's viper venom can clot blood, and a diluted version of it can stop uncontrolled bleeding in people suffering from **hemophilia**.

- The species' scientific name, *Daboia*, means "the lurker."

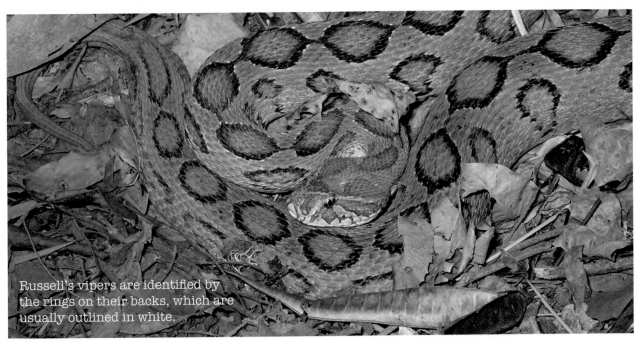
Russell's vipers are identified by the rings on their backs, which are usually outlined in white.

Glossary

camouflage On animals, colorings or markings that allow the animal to blend in with its surroundings.

carnivore An animal that eats meat.

echolocation The process used by animals and bats to locate prey; usually by calling to the air and whatever sound bounces of off objects, the animal can navigate around.

hemophilia A blood defect, mostly in males, that delays clotting and makes bleeding difficult to stop.

ligaments A tough band of tissue that holds bones together or keeps an organ in place in the body.

marsupials A type of animal that protects its babies in a pouch.

predator An animal that hunts other animals.

prey An animal picked by another animal to be its food.

scavengers Animals that eat other animals' leftovers.

scrublands Land that is covered with small bushes and trees.

species A group of plants of animals similar to each other that can produce other plants and animals.

venomous Poisonous.

Find Out More

Do you want to learn more about your favorite animals from this book? Check out these books and websites:

Books

Barr, Brady, and Kathleen Weidner Zoehfeld. *Crocodile Encounters: and More True Stories of Adventures with Animals.* Washington, DC: National Geographic, 2012.

Carney, Elizabeth. *Everything Big Cats.* Washington, DC: National Geographic, 2011.

Hughes, Catherine D. *National Geographic: Little Kids First Big Book of Animals.* Washington, DC: National Geographic, 2010.

Websites

National Geographic's Animal Profiles

kids.nationalgeographic.com/kids/animals

This website is great for looking up more facts about your favorite animals around the world.

Smithsonian National Zoo—Animal Facts

nationalzoo.si.edu/audiences/kids/facts.cfm

This website lists facts about many different animals that can be found at the National Zoo in Washington, DC.

Index